Weekend Knitting! ™

Merry Cables Scarf
page 22

Plum Berry Blanket & Pillow
page 32

Fun Family Mittens
page 14

D1303148

Table of Contents

Strut Your Stuff Sweater

Design by Bonnie Franz

Sizes

Dog's small (medium, large) Instructions are given for smallest size, with larger sizes in parentheses. When only 1 number is given, it applies to all sizes.

Finished Measurements

Back width: 14 (17, 20) inches

Length: 15 (19¾, 24¾) inches

Materials

- Plymouth Encore Chunky (bulky weight; 75% acrylic/25% wool; 143 yds/100g per skein): 1 (2, 2) skein(s) navy #658 (MC) and 1 skein grey #678 (CC
- Size 8 (5mm) circular needles at least 24 inches long
- Size 10 (6mm) circular needle at least 24 inches long, or size needed to obtain gauge
- Tapestry needle
- 3 (⅞-inch) buttons

Gauge

13 sts and 18 rows = 4 inches/10cm in St st with larger needles.

To save time, take time to check gauge.

Stripe Pattern

Work following sequence in St st:

5 rows MC, 1 row CC

Rep these 6 rows for pat.

Pattern Notes

This sweater is worked from side to side.

The circular needle allows you to work the Stripe Pattern from either side of fabric depending on where the necessary yarn is.

Dog Sweater

Back

Using smaller needles and MC, cast on 42 (58, 74) sts.

Knit 3 rows.

Buttonhole row: K16 (20, 26), k2tog, yo, knit to last 18 (22, 28) sts, yo, k2tog, knit to end of row.

Knit 3 rows.

Change to larger needles, and work even in St st and Stripe pat until piece measures 11 (14, 17) inches from beg.

Change to smaller needles and MC, and knit 6 rows.

Belly Band

Bind off 14 (18, 24) sts, k14 (18, 22), bind off rem 14 (18, 24) sts.

Work rem 14 (18, 22) sts in garter st until band measures approx 3½ (5, 6) inches or length needed to reach around belly of dog.

Bind off all sts.

Back & Front Edges

*With smaller needles and MC, pick up and knit 44 (58, 71) sts across back edge of sweater.

Knit 6 rows.*

Bind off all sts.

Rep from * to * across front edge of sweater.

Chest Strap

Next row: Bind off 38 (48, 56) sts, knit to end of row.

Continue in garter st until strap measures 6 (8, 10) inches, or length needed to reach around upper chest comfortably.

Buttonhole row: K2 (3, 4), yo, k2tog, knit to end of row.

Knit 4 rows.

Bind off all sts.

Finishing

Sew 2 buttons on Belly Band and 1 button on Chest Strap opposite buttonholes. ●

Rainy Day Reading Socks

Design by Victoria Light

Skill Level

■■■□ INTERMEDIATE

Sizes

Woman's small (medium, large) to fit shoe sizes 3–6 (6–9, 8–12)

Instructions are given for smallest size, with larger sizes in parentheses. When only 1 number is given, it applies to all sizes.

Finished Measurements

Circumference: 6½ (7¼, 8) inches

Length cuff to heel: Approx 6½ (7, 7½) inches

Length heel to toe: Approx 9 (10, 11) inches

Materials

- Berroco Vintage (worsted weight; 52% acrylic/40% wool/8% nylon; 218 yds/100g per hank): 1 hank each mocha #5103 (A), tang #5164 (B), fennel #5175 (C), Neptune #5197 (D), azure #5146 (E) and petunia #51105 (F)
- Size 6 (4mm) double-point needles (set of 5) or size needed to obtain gauge
- Size 8 (5mm) double-point needles or size needed to obtain gauge
- Stitch markers (4)
- Removable stitch marker

Gauge

24 sts and 26 rnds = 4 inches/10cm in 2x2 Rib with smaller needles, blocked.

22 sts and 24 rnds = 4 inches/10cm in 2-color stranded St st with larger needles, blocked.

To save time, take time to check gauge.

Special Abbreviations

N1, N2, N3, N4: Needle 1, Needle 2, Needle 3, Needle 4.

Pattern Stitches

2x2 Rib (multiple of 4 sts)

Rnd 1: *K2, p2; rep from * around.
Rep Rnd 1 for pat.

Stripe Pat A (multiple of 4 sts)

Rnds 1–6: *K2 A, k2 B; rep from * around.

Rnds 7–12: *K2 A, k2 F; rep from * around.

Rnds 13–17: *K2 A, k2 C; rep from * around.

Rnds 18–22: *K2 A, k2 E; rep from * around.

Rnds 23–27: *K2 A, k2 B; rep from * around.

Rnds 28–32: *K2 A, k2 D; rep from * around.

Rnds 33–37: *K2 A, k2 C; rep from * around.

Rnds 38–41: *K2 A, k2 F; rep from * around.

Rnds 42–45: *K2 A, k2 E; rep from * around.

Rnds 46–50: *K2 A, k2 B; rep from * around.

Rnds 51–56: *K2 A, k2 D; rep from * around.

Rnds 57–62: *K2 A, k2 C; rep from * around.

Stripe Pat B (multiple of 4 sts)

Rnds 1–6: *K2 A, k2 B; rep from * around.

Rnds 7–11: *K2 A, k2 C; rep from * around.

Rnds 12–16: *K2 A, k2 E; rep from * around.

Rnds 17–22: *K2 A, k2 F; rep from * around.

Rnds 23–27: *K2 A, k2 B; rep from * around.

Rnds 28–33: *K2 A, k2 D; rep from * around.

Rnds 34–39: *K2 A, k2 C; rep from * around.

Rnds 40–45: *K2 A, k2 F; rep from * around.

Rnds 46–51: *K2 A, k2 E; rep from * around.

Rnds 52–56: *K2 A, k2 B; rep from * around.

Rnds 57–62: *K2 A, k2 D; rep from * around.

Pattern Notes

Sock is worked from the cuff down, with an afterthought heel and a gathered toe.

Each sock is worked with a different color sequence. At each color change, cut yarn that is being discontinued.

Pattern is written for 5 double-point needles, but use whichever circular knitting method you prefer, whether it's working with 4 double-point needles, 2 circular needles, Magic Loop (with a long circular needle) or a short (9- to 12-inch) circular needle. If using a short circular needle, you'll have to switch to another method when working the toe and heel.

Socks

Sock A
Cuff

With smaller dpns and A, and using long-tail method, cast on 36 (40, 44) sts; mark beg of rnd and join, taking care not to twist sts. If desired, distribute sts so that there's a multiple of 4 sts on each dpn.

Work 2½ (3, 3½) inches in 2x2 Rib.

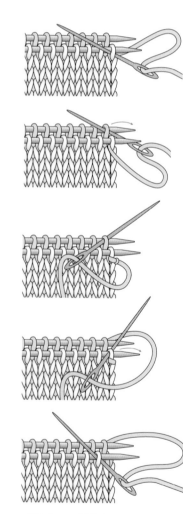

Long-Tail Cast-On

Make a slip knot on the right needle.

Place the thumb and index finger of your left hand between the yarn ends with the long yarn end over your thumb, and the strand from the yarn ball over your index finger. Close your other fingers over the strands to hold them against your palm. Spread your thumb and index fingers apart and draw the yarn into a V.

Place the needle in front of the strand around your thumb and bring it underneath this strand. Carry the needle over and under the strand on your index finger.

Draw the strand through the loop on your thumb. Drop the loop from your thumb and draw up the strand to form a stitch on the knitting needle.

Repeat until you have cast on the number of stitches indicated in the pattern.

Leg

Switch to larger dpns.

Work Rnds 1–27 of Stripe Pat A.

Afterthought heel row: With waste yarn, k18 (20, 22); slip sts just worked back to LH needle(s).

Foot

Work Rnds 28–62 of Stripe Pat A.

If necessary, rep Rnd 62 until foot measures just short of desired length.

Toe

Dec rnd: Alternating A and C, *k2tog; rep from * around; cut C—18 (20, 22) sts.

Next rnd: With A, *k2tog; rep from * around—9 (10, 11) sts.

Cut A, leaving a 10-inch tail.

Using tapestry needle, thread tail through rem sts, and pull tight.

Weave in all ends.

Afterthought Heel

Remove waste yarn and transfer live sts to 4 dpns; pm at center back leg for beg of rnd—36 (40, 44) sts with 9 (10, 11) sts per dpn; if necessary make an extra loop at one corner to achieve correct st count.

Rnd 1: Join B at beg of rnd and work as follows: N1: K9 (10, 11), then pick up and knit 1 st from sock edge; N2: pick up and knit 1 st, knit to end; N2 and N3: work as for N1 and N2—40 (44, 48) sts with 10 (11, 12) sts per dpn.

Dec rnd: N1: Knit to last 3 sts, k2tog, k1; N2: k1, ssk, knit to end; N3 and N4 work as for N1 and N2—36 (40, 44) sts.

Continuing in St st, rep Dec rnd [every other rnd] 5 (5, 6) times—16 (20, 20) sts.

Cut yarn, leaving a 12-inch tail.

Slip sts from N4 to N1 and from N3 to N2.

Close heel by grafting sts using Kitchener st.

Sock B

Work as for Sock A, but use Stripe Pat B.

Finishing

Weave in all ends.

Block.

Kitchener Stitch

Mix It Up Slippers

Designs by Laurie Gonyea

Skill Level

◨■◻◻ EASY

Sizes

Woman's small (medium, large)

Instructions are given for smallest size, with larger sizes in parentheses. When only 1 number is given, it applies to all sizes.

Finished Measurement

Length: 9 (10, 11) inches

Materials

- Plymouth Yarn Cleo (DK weight; 100% mercerized pima cotton; 125 yds/50g per skein): 2 skeins Cayman Bay #0165
- Size 5 (3.75mm) needles or size needed to obtain gauge
- Stitch markers

Gauge

28 sts and 24 rows = 4 inches/10cm in Whelk pat.

32 sts and 32 rows = 4 inches/10cm in Fractured Lattice pat.

40 sts and 24 rows = 4 inches/10cm in Quilted Cross-St pat.

Special Abbreviations

Left Twist (LT): Skip first st on LH needle, knit 2nd st tbl, knit first st and slip both sts off needles.

Right Twist (RT): K2tog keeping both sts on needle, knit first st.

Pattern Stitches

Whelk (multiple of 4 sts + 3)

Note: *A chart is provided for those preferring to work Whelk pat from a chart.*

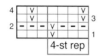

WHELK CHART

STITCH KEY
☐ K on RS, p on WS
▭ P on RS, k on WS
Ⅴ Sl 1

Row 1 (RS): K3, *sl 1, k3; rep from * across.

Row 2: Rep Row 1.

Row 3: K1, *sl 1, k3; rep from * to last 2 sts, sl 1, k1.

Row 4: P1, *sl 1, p3; rep from * to last 2 sts, sl 1, p1.

Rep Rows 1–4 for pat.

Fractured Lattice (multiple of 8 sts + 8)

Note: *A chart is provided for those preferring to work Fractured Lattice pat from a chart.*

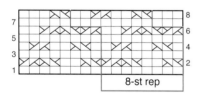

FRACTURED LATTICE CHART

STITCH KEY
☐ K on RS, p on WS
⧗ LT
⧗ RT

Row 1 (WS) and all other WS rows: Purl.

Row 2 (RS): *LT, k2, LT, RT; rep from * across.

Row 4: *K1, LT, k2, RT, k1; rep from * across.

Row 6: *RT, LT, RT, k2; rep from * across.

Row 8: K3, *LT, k2, RT, k2; rep from * to last 5 sts, LT, k3.

Rep Rows 1–8 for pat.

Quilted Cross-St (multiple of 4 sts + 4)

Rows 1 and 3 (WS): *P1, k1; rep from * across.

Row 2 (RS): *P1, sl 1 kwise, kfb, k1, pass slipped st over last 3 sts made; rep from * across.

Row 4: P1, k1, *p1, sl 1 kwise, kfb, k1, pass slipped st over last 3 sts made; rep from * to last 2 sts, p1, k1.

Rep Rows 1–4 for pat.

Pattern Notes

Slippers are shown in Whelk pattern. Instructions are included for slippers using 2 additional pattern stitches.

Unless specified otherwise, slip stitches purlwise with yarn held to the wrong side.

An attached I-cord edging is formed as follows: Knit 3 at beginning of every row and slip last 3 stitches purlwise with the yarn in front.

Whelk Slippers

Cast on 57 sts.

Row 1 (RS): K3, pm, work Row 1 of Whelk pat to last 3 sts, pm, sl 3 wyif.

Continuing to work first and last 3 sts as I-cord edging and center sts in Whelk pat, work even until piece measures 7 (8, 9) inches, ending with a WS row.

Next row: K3, p1, *k1, p1; rep from * to marker, sl 3 wyif.

Next row: K3, k1, *p1, k1; rep from * to marker, sl 3 wyif.

Rep last 2 rows until slipper measures 9 (10, 11) inches, ending with a WS row and removing markers on last row.

Shape Toe

Row 1 (RS): *K2, k2tog; rep from * to last st, k1—43 sts.

Rows 2, 4 and 6: Purl.

Row 3: *K1, k2tog; rep from * to last st, k1—29 sts.

Row 5: *K2tog; rep from * to last st, k1—15 sts.

Row 7: *K2tog; rep from * to last st, k1—8 sts.

Cut yarn, leaving an 18-inch tail. Using tapestry needle, thread tail through rem sts and pull tight.

Fractured Lattice Slippers

Cast on 62 sts.

Row 1 (RS): K3, pm, work Row 1 of Fractured Lattice pat to last 3 sts, pm, sl 3 wyif.

Continuing to work first and last 3 sts as I-cord edging and center sts in Fractured Lattice pat, work even until piece measures 7 (8, 9) inches, ending with a WS row.

Next row (RS): K3, *p1, k1; rep from * to marker, sl 3 wyif.

Rep last row until slipper measures 9 (10, 11) inches, ending with a WS row and removing markers on last row.

Shape Toe

Row 1 (RS): *K2, k2tog; rep from * to last 2 sts, k2—47 sts.

Rows 2, 4 and 6: Purl.

Row 3: *K1, k2tog; rep from * to last 2 sts, k2—32 sts.

Row 5: *K2tog; rep from * across—16 sts.

Row 7: *K2tog; rep from * across—8 sts.

Cut yarn, leaving an 18-inch tail.

Finish same as for Whelk Slippers.

Quilted Cross-Stitch Slippers

Cast on 74 sts.

Row 1 (RS): K3, pm, work Row 1 of Quilted Cross-St pat to last 3 sts, pm, sl 3 wyif.

Continuing to work first and last 3 sts as I-cord edging and center sts in Quilted Cross-St pat, work even until piece measures 7 (8, 9) inches, ending with a WS row.

Next row (RS): K3, *p1, k1; rep from * to marker, sl 3 wyif.

Rep last row until slipper measures 9 (10, 11) inches, ending with a WS row and removing markers on last row.

Shape Toe

Row 1 (RS): *K2, k2tog; rep from * to last 2 sts, k2—56 sts.

Rows 2, 4 and 6: Purl.

Row 3: *K1, k2tog; rep from * to last 2 sts, k2—38 sts.

Row 5: *K2tog; rep from * across—19 sts.

Row 7: *K2tog; rep from * to last st, k1—10 sts.

Cut yarn, leaving an 18-inch tail.

Finish same as for Whelk Slippers.

Finishing

Using tail, sew approx 2½ inches from toe along top of slipper. Secure yarn by weaving through several sts on WS and then cut.

Fold slipper in half lengthwise and sew heel edges tog to close slipper.

Weave in ends. ●

Chamomile Poncho

Design by Lena Skvagerson for Annie's Signature Designs

Skill Level

 EASY

Finished Measurements

Approx 35 inches deep (from neck to bottom point) x 58½ inches wide (wingspan)

Materials

- Red Heart Unforgettable (worsted weight; 100% acrylic; 270 yds/100g per ball): 2 balls each polo #3956 (A) and echo #3940 (B) **[4 MEDIUM]**
- Size 10 (6mm) 24-inch or longer circular needle or size needed to obtain gauge
- Removable stitch markers

Gauge

16 sts and 24 rows = 4 inches/10cm in pat st, blocked.

To save time, take time to check gauge.

Special Abbreviation

Make 1 Left (M1L): Insert LH needle from front to back under horizontal strand between last st worked and next st on LH needle; knit through back of resulting loop.

Make 1 Right (M1R): Insert LH needle from back to front under horizontal strand between last st worked and next st on LH needle; knit into front of resulting loop.

Pattern Notes

Poncho is comprised of 2 identical asymmetrical triangles that are sewn together leaving a neck opening.

Three selvage stitches are worked in garter at beginning and end of each row throughout the pattern.

All slip stitches are worked with the yarn held to the right side of the fabric.

Circular needle is used on the body to accommodate large number of stitches. Do not join; work back and forth in rows.

Be sure to interlock the yarns at each color change to prevent holes.

Poncho

Triangle

Make 2.

With A, cast on 6 sts.

Rows 1–3: Knit.

Row 4 (RS): K3, M1R, M1L, k3—8 sts.

Row 5: K3, p2, k3.

Row 6: Knit to last 3 sts, M1L, k3—9 sts.

Row 7: K4, sl 2 wyib, change to B, k3.

Row 8: K5, p1, M1L, k3—10 sts.

Row 9: K5, sl 2 wyib, change to A, k3.

Row 10: K5, p2, M1L, k3—11 sts.

Row 11: K3, p1, k2, sl 2 wyib, change to B, k3.

Row 12: K5, p2, k1, M1L, k3—12 sts.

Row 13: K3, sl 2 wyib, k2, sl 2 wyib, change to A, k3.

Row 14: K5, p2, k2, M1L, k3—13 sts.

Row 15: K4, sl 2 wyib, k2, sl 2 wyib, change to B, k3.

Row 16: K5, p2, k2, p1, M1L, k3—14 sts.

Row 17: K5, sl 2 wyib, k2, sl 2 wyib, change to A, k3.

Row 18: K3, [k2, p2] twice, M1L, k3—15 sts.

Row 19: K3, p1, [k2, sl 2 wyib] twice, change to B, k3.

Row 20: K3, [k2, p2] twice, k1, M1L, k3—16 sts.

Row 21: K3, [sl 2 wyib, k2] twice, sl 2 wyib, change to A, k3.

Row 22: K5, [p2, k2] twice, M1L, k3—17 sts.

Row 23: K4, [sl 2 wyib, k2] twice, sl 2 wyib, change to B, k3.

Row 24: K5, [p2, k2] twice, p1, M1L, k3—18 sts.

Row 25: K3, *k2, sl 2 wyib; rep from * to last 3 sts, change to A, k3.

Row 26: K3, [k2, p2] to last 3 sts, M1L, k3—19 sts.

Row 27: K3, p1, *k2, sl 2 wyib; rep from * to last 3 sts, change to B, k3.

Row 28: K3, [k2, p2] to last 4 sts, k1, M1L, k3—20 sts.

Row 29: K3, sl 2 wyib, *k2, sl 2 wyib; rep from * to last 3 sts, change to A, k3.

Row 30: K3, [k2, p2] to last 5 sts, k2, M1L, k3—21 sts.

Row 31: K4, sl 2 wyib, *k2, sl 2 wyib; rep from * to last 3 sts, change to B, k3.

Row 32: K3, [k2, p2] to last 6 sts, k2, p1, M1L, k3—22 sts.

Rep Rows 25–32, continuing to inc 1 st on every RS row and change colors as established, until there are 144 sts and piece measures 46 inches along the straight edge, ending with a WS row.

Knit 4 rows.

Bind off.

Finishing

Lay 1 triangle on top of the other with WS facing each other as shown on Assembly Diagram.

Mark center 13½ inches for neck opening on side of triangle that measures 58½ inches. Sew from neck edge out 9 inches on each side, forming shoulder seams; leave the rem 13½ inches of each side unsewn.

Weave in ends. Block to measurements. ●

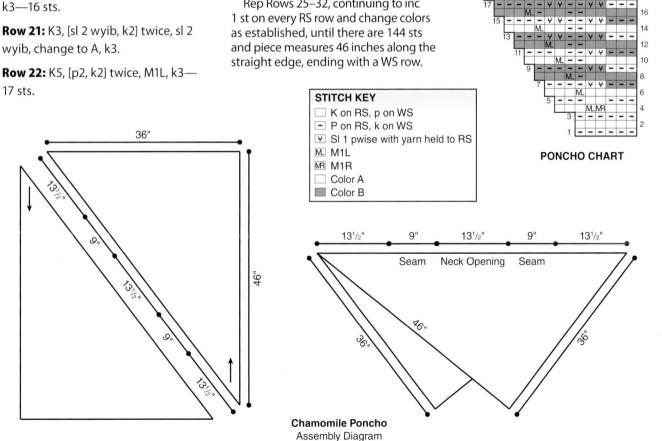

STITCH KEY
- ☐ K on RS, p on WS
- − P on RS, k on WS
- ⋎ Sl 1 pwise with yarn held to RS
- M̲L̲ M1L
- M̲R̲ M1R
- ☐ Color A
- ▨ Color B

PONCHO CHART

4-st rep

8-row rep

Chamomile Poncho
Assembly Diagram
Note: Arrows indicate direction of work.

Beguiling Basket-Weave Cap & Scarf

Designs by Lena Skvagerson for Annie's Signature Designs

Skill Level

■■□□ EASY

Sizes

Hat

Woman's small/medium (medium/large)

Instructions are given for smaller size, with larger size in parentheses. When only 1 number is given, it applies to both sizes.

Finished Measurements

Hat

Circumference: 17¾ (19½) inches (unstretched)

Height: 10 (10½) inches

Scarf

9 inches x 70 inches

Materials

- Worsted weight yarn (100% acrylic): 180 yds/100g gray heather for both sizes of hat; 540 yds/300g gray heather for scarf
- Size 8 (5mm) straight, 16-inch circular and double-point needles (set of 5) or size needed to obtain gauge
- Stitch markers

Gauge

18 sts and 27 rnds/rows = 4 inches/10cm in Basket Weave pat, blocked.

To save time, take time to check gauge.

Special Abbreviations

Make 1 Left (M1L): Insert LH needle from front to back under horizontal strand between last st worked and next st on LH needle; knit through back of resulting loop.

Make 1 Right (M1R): Insert LH needle from back to front under horizontal strand between last st worked and next st on LH needle; knit into front of resulting loop.

Pattern Stitches

2 x 2 Rib (multiple of 4 sts)

All rnds: *K2, p2; rep from * around.

Basket Weave (multiple of 4 sts; worked in rnds)

Rnds 1 and 2: Purl.

Rnd 3: Knit.

Rnds 4 and 5: *K2, p2; rep from * around.

Rnd 6: Knit.

Rnds 7 and 8: Purl.

Rnd 9: Knit.

Rnds 10 and 11: *P2, k2; rep from * around.

Rnd 12: Knit.

Rep Rnds 1–12 for pat.

Basket Weave (multiple of 4 sts; worked in rows)

Row 1 (RS): Purl.

Rows 2 and 3: Knit.

Rows 4 and 5: *P2, k2; rep from * across.

Rows 6 and 7: Purl.

Rows 8 and 9: Knit.

Rows 10 and 11: *K2, p2; rep from * across.

Row 12: Purl.

Rep Rows 1–12 for pat.

Hat

With circular needle, cast on 80 (88) sts; pm for beg of rnd and join without twisting.

Work 5 (7) rnds in 2 x 2 Rib.

Work [12-rnd Basket Weave pat] 4 times.

Shape Crown

Note: Change to dpns when sts no longer fit comfortably on circular needle.

Rnd 1: *P8 (9), p2tog; rep from * around—72 (80) sts.

Rnd 2: Purl.

Rnd 3: *K2tog, k7 (8); rep from * around—64 (72) sts.

Rnds 4 and 5: *K2, p2; rep from * around.

Rnd 6: *K6 (7), k2tog; rep from * around—56 (64) sts.

Rnd 7: *P2tog, p5 (6); rep from * around—48 (56) sts.

Rnd 8: *P4 (5), p2tog; rep from * around—40 (48) sts.

Rnd 9: *K2tog, p3 (4); rep from * around—32 (40) sts.

Rnds 11 and 12: *P2, k2; rep from * around.

Rnd 13: *K2 (3), k2tog; rep from * around—24 (32) sts.

Rnd 14: *P2tog, p1 (2); rep from * around—16 (24) sts.

Rnd 15: P2tog around—8 (12) sts.

Size Medium/Large Only
Rnd 16: K2tog around—6 sts.

Both Sizes
Cut yarn, leaving an 8-inch tail.

Using tapestry needle, thread tail through rem sts and pull tight.

Finishing
Weave in ends.

Scarf

Ribbed Border
Cast on 44 sts.

Row 1 (RS): K5, pm; k2, [p2, k2] 8 times, pm; k5.

Row 2: K5; p2, [k2, p2] 8 times; k5.

Rep Rows 1 and 2 until scarf measures 7 inches, ending with Row 1.

Body
Next row (WS, dec): K5; k2tog, knit to last 7 sts, ssk; k5—42 sts.

Set-up row (RS): K5; work Basket Weave pat to last 5 sts; k5.

Keeping 5 sts at each side in garter st, continue in Basket Weave pat until scarf measures approx 63 inches, ending with Pat Row 2 or 8.

Next row (RS, inc): K5, M1R, purl to last 5 sts, M1L, k5—44 sts.

Ribbed Border
Beg with a WS row, work as for first border until rib measures 7 inches.

Bind off in rib.

Finishing
Weave in ends.

Block lightly if desired. ●

Fun Family Mittens

Design by Christine L. Walter

Skill Level

■■■□ INTERMEDIATE

Sizes

Child's (woman's, man's)

Instructions are given for smallest size, with larger sizes in parentheses. When only 1 number is given, it applies to all sizes.

Finished Measurement

Hand circumference: 6 (8, 9) inches

Materials

- Worsted weight yarn (100% wool): 210 yds/100g salmon (child's) or turquoise (woman's/man's)
- Size 6 (4mm) double-pointed needles or size needed to obtain gauge
- Stitch markers (1 in CC for beg of rnd)
- Tapestry needle

Gauge

23 sts and 30 rows = 4 inches/10cm in Waffle Rib pat (blocked).

To save time, take time to check gauge.

Special Abbreviations

M1L (Make 1 Left): Insert LH needle from front to back under the horizontal strand between the last st worked and next st on left needle. With RH needle, knit into the back of this loop.

M1R (Make 1 Right): Insert LH needle from back to front under the horizontal strand between the last st worked and next st on left needle. With RH needle, knit into the front of this loop.

Pm (Place Marker): Place marker on needle.

Inc (Increase): Knit in front and back of st to inc 1 st.

Pattern Stitch

Waffle Rib (multiple of 5 sts)

Rnds 1 and 2: Knit.

Rnds 3–6: *K1, p3, k1; rep from * to end.
  Rep Rows 1–6 for pat.

Mittens

Cuff

Cast on 30 (40, 50) sts. Distribute evenly on 3 or 4 dpns and join without twisting; pm between first and last sts.

  Work in k1, p1 rib until cuff measures 2¼ (2¾, 3) inches.

Thumb Gusset

Work Rnd 1 of Waffle Rib across 15 (20, 25) sts, pm, k1, pm, continue in pat to last st, inc1. (31, 41, 51 sts)

Inc rnd: Work in pat to first marker, sl marker; M1L, knit to next marker, M1R, sl marker; work in pat to end of rnd.

  Rep Inc rnd [every 3rd rnd] 2 (5, 7) times, then [every 4th rnd] 2 (1, 0) times. (11, 15, 17 sts between markers)

Next rnd: Work in pat to first marker, place sts between markers on a piece of waste yarn (removing markers), cast on 1 st over gap left by gusset, work in pat to end of rnd. (31, 41, 51 sts)

Hand

Next rnd: Work in pat as established, knitting the st cast on over gusset.

Next rnd: Work 15 (20, 25) sts in pat, k2tog, work in pat to end of rnd. (30, 40, 50 sts)

  Work even until piece measures approx 3½ (5¾, 6¾) inches from top of ribbing.

Next rnd: Work 15 (20, 25) sts in pat, pm, work to end of rnd.

Shape Top

Dec rnd: *Ssk, work in pat as established to 2 sts before marker, k2tog, sl marker; rep from *. (26, 36, 46 sts)

Next rnd: *K1, work in pat to 1 st before marker, k1; rep from *.
  [Rep last 2 rnds] 3 (4, 6) times. (14, 20, 22 sts)

Next rnd: *Ssk, knit to 2 sts before marker, k2tog, sl marker; rep from *. (10, 16, 18 sts)
  [Rep last rnd] 1 (2, 3) time(s). (6, 8, 6 sts)

Thumb

Place 11 (15, 17) gusset sts onto 3 dpn; pick up and knit 1 st over gap and join; pm for beg of rnd. (12, 16, 18 sts)

  Work in St st until thumb measures approx 1 (1¾, 2) inches from pick-up rnd.

Next rnd: [K4 (5, 6), pm] twice, k4 (6, 6).

Shape Top

Dec rnd: [Knit to 2 sts before marker, k2tog] around. (9, 13, 15 sts)
  Rep Dec rnd [every (every other, every other) rnd] 1 (2, 2) time(s). (6, 7, 9 sts)

Largest Size Only

Rep Dec rnd. (6 sts)

All Sizes

Cut yarn, leaving a 5-inch tail.
  Using tapestry needle, thread tail through rem sts and pull tight.

Finishing

Weave in ends.
  Block lightly. ●

Windowpanes of Color Beanie

Design by Edie Eckman

Skill Level

◼◼◼◻ INTERMEDIATE

Size

Fits 22–23-inch-circumference head

Finished Measurements

Circumference: 19 inches (unstretched)

Height: Approx 9½ inches

Materials

- Patons Classic Wool (worsted weight; 100% wool; 194 yds/ 100g per ball): 1 ball each dark gray mix #00225 (A), pumpkin #77605 (B), purple night #77782 (C) and sprout #77759 (D)
- Size 7 (4.5mm) 16-inch circular and double-point needles or size needed to obtain gauge
- Stitch marker

Gauge

20 sts and 32 rows = 4 inch/10cm in Windowpane Stripe pat.

To save time, take time to check gauge.

Pattern Stitch

Windowpane Stripe

Rnd 1: With A, knit around.

Rnd 2: Purl around.

Rnds 3 and 4: With B, [k3, sl 1] around.

Rnds 5 and 6: With A, rep Rnds 1 and 2.

Rnds 7 and 8: With D, rep Rnds 3 and 4.

Rnds 9 and 10: With A, rep Rnds 1 and 2.

Rnds 11 and 12: With C, rep Rnds 3 and 4.

Rep Rnds 1–12 for pat.

Pattern Note

Slip all stitches purlwise unless otherwise stated.

Beanie

Body

With circular needle and A, cast on 96 sts. Place marker for beg of rnd and join, being careful not to twist sts.

Rnd 1: Purl around.

Rnd 2: With B, [k3, sl 1] around.

Rnd 3: [P3, sl 1 wyib] around.

Rnd 4: With A, knit around.

Rnd 5: Purl around.

Rnd 6: With C, [k1, sl 1, k2] around.

Rnd 7: [P1, sl 1 wyib, p2] around.

Rnd 8: With A, knit around.

Rnd 9: Purl around.

Rnds 10 and 11: With D, rep Rnd 2.

Rnds 12 and 13: With B, rep Rnds 6 and 7.

Rnds 14 and 15: With C, rep Rnd 2.

Work [Rnds 1–12 of Windowpane Stripe pat] twice.

Work Rnds 1–6 of Windowpane Stripe pat.

Shape Top

Note: *Change to dpns, as necessary, when sts no longer fit comfortably on circular needle.*

Rnd 1: With D, knit around.

Rnd 2: [K4, ssk] around—80 sts.

Rnd 3: With A, knit around.

Rnd 4: Purl around.

Rnd 5: With C, knit around.

Rnd 6: [K3, k2tog] around—64 sts.

Rnds 7 and 8: Rep Rnds 3 and 4.

Rnd 9: With B, knit around.

Rnd 10: [K2, ssk] around—48 sts.

Rnd 11: With A, knit around.

Rnd 12: [P1, p2tog] around—32 sts.

Rnd 13: With D, knit around.

Rnd 14: [K2tog] around—16 sts.

Rnd 15: With A, knit around.

Rnd 16: [P2tog] around—8 sts.

Cut yarn, leaving a long end. Weave end through rem sts. Pull tight to close circle. ●

Simple Cable Hat & Fingerless Mitts

Designs by Nazanin S. Fard

Skill Level

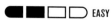 EASY

Finished Sizes

Hat: Fits adult average

Fingerless Gloves: Fits woman's average

Materials

- Worsted weight yarn (100% wool): 332 yds/200g tangerine for set
- Size 8 (5mm) 16-inch circular needle and set of 4 double-pointed needles or size needed to obtain gauge
- Stitch markers
- Cable needle
- Tapestry needle

Gauge

19 sts and 26 rnds = 4 inches/10cm in St st.

To save time, take time to check gauge.

Special Abbreviations

C6F (Cable 6 Front): Sl 3 sts to cn and hold in front, k3, k3 from cn.

C6B (Cable 6 Back): Sl 3 sts to cn and hold in back, k3, k3 from cn.

Pattern Stitch

Cable Pat (multiple of 20 sts)

Rnd 1: *K2, [p2, k6] twice, p2; rep from * around.

Rnd 2: *K2, p2, C6F, p2, C6B, p2; rep from * around.

Rnds 3–6: Rep Rnd 1.
　Rep Rnds 1–6 for pat.

Pattern Note

When working hat, change to double-point needles when stitches no longer fit comfortably on circular needle.

Hat

With circular needle, cast on 120 sts. Place marker for beg of rnd and join without twisting sts.

　Work K2, P2 Rib for 3 inches.

　Work Cable pat for approx 8 inches or desired length, ending with Rnd 3.

Crown

Rnd 1: *K2, p2, [k2tog] 3 times, p2tog, [k2tog] 3 times, p2; rep from * around. (78 sts)

Rnd 2: *K2, p2, k3, k2tog, k2, p2; rep from * around. (72 sts)

Rnds 3 and 4: *K2, p2, k6, p2; rep from * around.

Rnd 5: *K2, p2, C6B, p2; rep from * around.

Rnd 6: Rep Rnd 3.

Rnds 7–9: K2tog around. (9 sts)

　Cut yarn, leaving a 6-inch tail.

　Using tapestry needle, thread tail through rem sts and pull tight.

　Weave in all ends.

Fingerless Gloves

Right Hand

Cast on 48 sts.

　Distribute evenly on 3 dpns; place marker for beg of rnd and join without twisting sts.

　Work K2, P2 Rib for 3 inches.

Set-up Pat

Rnd 1: [K6, p2] twice, k2, p2, k22, p2, k2, p2.

Rnd 2: C6F, p2, C6B, p2, k2, p2, k22, p2, k2, p2.

Rnds 3–6: Rep Rnd 1.

　Rep [Rnds 1–6] until piece measures approx 5 inches or desired length to thumb opening.

Next rnd (thumb opening): Work in pat as established for 20 sts, bind off 4 sts, work to end of rnd.

Next rnd: Work in pat as established, casting on 4 sts over bound-off sts.

Work even until piece measures approx 7 inches or desired length, ending with Rnd 3.

Next rnd: *K1, k2tog twice, k1, p2; rep from * once more, then work in pat as established to end of rnd.

Bind off in pat.

Left Hand
Work same as Right Hand to thumb opening.

Next rnd (thumb opening): Work in pat as established for 38 sts, bind off 4 sts, work to end of rnd.

Complete as for Right Hand.

Finishing
Weave in all ends. ●

Cozy Cabin Cowl

Design by Cheryl Murray

Skill Level

 INTERMEDIATE

Finished Measurements

Circumference: 29 inches (bottom), 24 inches (top)

Width: 10½ inches

Materials

- Plymouth Yarn Encore (worsted weight; 75% acrylic/25% wool; 200 yds/100g per ball): 1 ball each dark wedgewood #598 (A), light wedgewood #514 (B) and green gremlin #0451 (C)
- Size 8 (5mm) knitting needles or size needed to obtain gauge
- Spare knitting needle, size 8 or 9
- Stitch holders or scrap yarn

Gauge

16 sts and 32 rows = 4 inches/10cm in garter st.

To save time, take time to check gauge.

Special Abbreviation

Wrap and Turn (W&T): Sl next st pwise to RH needle. Bring yarn between needles to opposite side of fabric, then sl same st back to LH needle. Turn, leaving rem sts unworked, then beg working back in the other direction.

Note: *There is no need to hide wraps on subsequent rows.*

Pattern Note

The cowl is worked flat in garter st, beginning with a center rectangle. Stitches are picked up along the sides of this and subsequent rectangles at a rate of 1 stitch for each ridge to create additional sections; arrows in the diagram indicate the direction of knitting. The final sections are shaped with short rows to create additional width at the lower edge.

Cowl

Section 1

With A and using long-tail cast-on (see page 6), cast on 10 sts.

Knit 18 rows (10 ridges). Cut A.

With B, knit 20 rows (10 ridges). Cut B.

With A, knit 20 rows (10 ridges).

Place sts on holder.

Section 2

With RS facing and C, pick up and knit 30 sts along 1 long side of Section 1.

Knit 19 rows (10 ridges).

Cut C and place sts on holder.

Rep on opposite edge.

Section 3

With RS facing and B, pick up and knit 10 sts along side of Section 2; knit 10 sts from holder; pick up and knit 10 sts along side of Section 2—30 sts.

Knit 31 rows (16 ridges). Cut B.

With C, knit 16 rows (8 ridges).

Cut C and place sts on holder.

Rep on opposite edge.

Section 4

With RS facing and A, pick up and knit 24 sts along side of Section 3; knit 30 sts from holder; pick up and knit 24 sts along side of Section 3—78 sts.

Knit 15 rows (8 ridges).

Bind off all sts kwise.

Rep on opposite edge.

Section 5 (Right Side)

With RS facing and A, pick up and knit 8 sts along side of Section 4; knit 30 sts from holder; pick up and knit 8 sts along side of Section 4—46 sts.

Knit 13 rows (7 ridges).

Short-row set 1 (RS): Knit to last 3 sts, W&T; **(WS):** knit to end.

Short-row set 2 (RS): Knit to 4 sts before previous wrapped st, W&T; **(WS):** knit to end.

Rep Short-row set 2 until all sts are worked.

Knit 1 row.

Place sts on holder.

Section 5 (Left Side)

With RS facing and A, pick up and knit 8 sts along side of Section 4; knit 30 sts from holder; pick up and knit 8 sts along side of Section 4—46 sts.

Knit 14 rows (7 ridges).

Short-row set 1 (WS): Knit to last 3 sts, W&T; **(RS):** knit to end.

Short-row set 2 (WS): Knit to 4 sts before previous wrapped st, W&T; **(RS):** knit to end.

Rep Short-row set 2 until all sts are worked.

Knit 1 row, then leave sts on needle.

Finishing

Holding RS tog, join the 2 sets of Section 5 live sts using 3-needle bind-off (see page 41).

Weave in all ends.

Block lightly if desired. ●

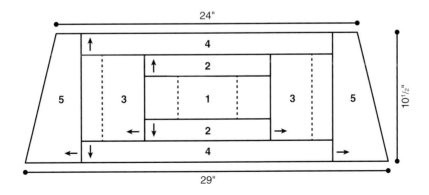

Cozy Cabin Cowl
Cowl Diagram
Note: Arrows indicate direction of knitting.

Merry Cables Scarf

Design by Laura Andersson

Skill Level

 INTERMEDIATE

Finished Measurements

6 inches wide; length as desired
[samples are 44 (54, 72) inches]

Materials

- Super chunky weight yarn (30% mohair/ 30% wool/40% acrylic): 168 yds pink; 224 yds aqua; 280 yds yellow

6 SUPER BULKY

- Size 11 (8mm) straight needles or size needed to obtain gauge
- Cable needle
- Tapestry needle

Gauge

11 sts and 14 rows = 4 inches/10cm in Seed St.

To save time, take time to check gauge.

Special Abbreviations

RT (Right Twist): K2tog, leaving sts on LH needle; insert RH needle from the front between the 2 sts just knitted tog, and knit the first st again; sl both sts from the needle tog.

C6B (Cable 6 Back): Sl 3 to cn and hold in back, k3, k3 from cn.

C6F (Cable 6 Front): Sl 3 sts to cn and hold in Front, k3, k3 sts from cn.

Pattern Stitch

Seed St (odd number of sts)

Row 1: *K1, p1; rep from * to last st, end k1.

Rep Row 1 for Seed St.

Pattern Note

This scarf is reversible with a 9-stitch center cable on the right side and 2-stitch mini-cables at the sides on the wrong side.

Scarf

Cast on 17 sts.

Edge

Work in Seed St for 2 inches, inc 5 sts evenly across last row. (23 sts)

Main Scarf Panel

Row 1 (RS): P1, k1, p2, k1, p2, k9, p2, k1, p2, k1, p1.

Row 2 and all WS rows: K1, p1, RT, p1, k2, p9, k2, p1, RT, p1, k1.

Row 3: P1, k1, p2, k1, p2, C6F, k3, p2, k1, p2, k1, p1.

Row 5: Rep Row 1.

Row 7: P1, k1, p2, k1, p2, k3, C6B, p2, k1, p2, k1, p1.

Row 8: Rep Row 2.

Rep Rows 1–8 until scarf is 2 inches short of desired length, ending with Row 1 or 5.

Edge

Next row (WS): Work in Seed St, dec 5 sts evenly across first row in pat. (17 sts)

Continue in Seed St for 2 inches.

Bind off in pat.

Finishing

Weave in all ends.

Gently hand-wash the scarf in lukewarm water and dry flat. ●

Wanderlust Cap

Design by Christine L. Walter

Skill Level

 EASY

Finished Sizes

Fits adult's small (adult's large)

Finished Measurement

Fits head circumference of 18–20 inches (20–22 inches)

Materials

- Worsted weight yarn (100% wool): 223 yds/100g tan (large hat)
- Worsted weight yarn (51% cotton/49% acrylic): 214 yds/100g coral (small hat)
- Size 8 (5mm) 16-inch circular needle and set of double-pointed needles or size needed to obtain gauge (large hat)
- Size 6 (4mm) 16-inch circular and set of double-pointed needles or size needed to obtain gauge (small hat)
- Stitch marker
- Tapestry needle

Gauge

Small Hat: 23 sts and 32 rnds = 4 inches/10cm in K2, P2 Rib (slightly stretched) using smaller needles.

Large Hat: 21 sts and 28 rnds = 4 inches/10cm in K2, P2 Rib (slightly stretched) using larger needles.

To save time, take time to check gauge.

Pattern Notes

Hat sizes are adjusted by changing needle size and gauge; both sizes use the same number of stitches and rounds.

Change to double-point needles when stitches no longer fit comfortably on circular needle.

Wavy Rib pattern will be continued to end of crown shaping.

Pattern Stitches

A. K2, P2 Rib

Rnd 1: K1, *p2, k2; rep from * ending k1.
Rep Rnd 1 for pat.

B. Wavy Rib (multiple of 16)

Rnds 1, 3, 5 and 7: *K9, p2, k2, p2, k1; rep from * around.

Rnds 2, 4, 6 and 8: *K1, p6, [k2, p2] twice, k1; rep from * around.

Rnds 9, 11, 13 and 15: *K1, p2, k2, p2, k9; rep from * around.

Rnds 10, 12, 14 and 16: *K1, [p2, k2] twice, p6, k1; rep from * around.
Rep Rnds 1–16 for pat.

Hat

Using appropriate-sized needle, cast on 112 sts; place marker for beg of rnd and join without twisting sts.

Work 28 rnds in K2, P2 Rib or until cuff is desired length (it will be folded back doubled).

Work 32 rnds of Wavy Rib.

Crown

Rnd 1: *K9, p2, k2, p1, k2tog; rep from * around. (105 sts)

Rnd 2: *K1, p6, k2, p2, k2, k2tog; rep from * around. (98 sts)

Rnd 3: *K9, p2, k1, k2tog; rep from * around. (91 sts)

Rnd 4: *K1, p6, k2, p2, k2tog; rep from * around. (84 sts)

Rnd 5: *K9, p1, k2tog; rep from * around. (77 sts)

Rnd 6: *K1, p6, k2, k2tog; rep from * around. (70 sts)

Rnd 7: *K8, k2tog; rep from * around. (63 sts)

Rnd 8: *K1, p6, k2tog; rep from * around. (56 sts)

Rnd 9: *K1, p2, k2, p1, k2tog; rep from * around. (49 sts)

Rnd 10: *K1, p2, k2, k2tog; rep from * around. (42 sts)

Rnd 11: *K1, p2, k1, k2tog; rep from * around. (35 sts)

Rnd 12: *K1, p2, k2tog; rep from * around. (28 sts)

Rnd 13: *K1, p1, k2tog; rep from * around. (21 sts)

Rnd 14: *K1, k2tog; rep from * around. (14 sts)

Rnd 15: *K2tog; rep from * around. (7 sts)

Cut yarn, leaving an 8-inch tail.

Using tapestry needle, thread tail through rem sts twice, and pull tight.

Finishing

Weave in ends. Block hat lightly using steam and let dry. ●

Baby Cable Slippers

Design by Amy Niezur

Skill Level

 INTERMEDIATE

Size

Adult

Finished Measurement

Foot circumference: 8 inches

Materials

- Worsted weight yarn (50% silk/ 50% wool): 220 yds/100g red
- Size 6 (4mm) double-point needles or size needed to obtain gauge
- Stitch holder
- Stitch marker

Gauge

20 sts and 28 rows = 4 inches/10cm in pat.

To save time, take time to check gauge.

Special Abbreviations

N1, N2, N3, N4: Needle 1, Needle 2, Needle 3, Needle 4.

Pattern Stitch

Baby Cable (multiple of 4 sts)

Rnds 1–3: *K2, p2; rep from * around.

Rnd 4: *K2tog, leave sts on LH needle, insert tip of RH needle back into first st, k1, sl sts off needle, p2; rep from * around.

Rep Rnds 1–4 for pat.

Pattern Note

Slip all stitches purlwise.

Slipper

Leg

Cast on 40 sts, divide on dpn, place marker for beg of rnd and join without twisting.

Work in Baby Cable pat for 4 inches, ending with Rnd 4 of pat.

Heel flap

K8, turn. P18. These sts will form heel flap. Place rem 22 instep sts on holder. Heel flap is worked back and forth in rows.

Row 1: *Sl 1, k1; rep from * across.

Row 2: Sl 1, purl across.

Rows 3–18: Rep Rows 1 and 2.

There will be 9 edge-chain sts along each side of heel flap.

Heel turn

Row 1: K11, ssk, k1, turn.

Row 2: Sl 1, p5, p2tog, p1, turn.

Row 3: Sl 1, knit to 1 st before gap, ssk (taking 1 st from each side of gap), k1, turn.

Row 4: Sl 1, purl to 1 st before gap, p2tog (taking 1 st from each side of gap), p1, turn.

Rep Rows 3 and 4 until all heel sts have been worked, ending with a WS row—2 sts.

Gusset

Set-up rnd: N1: knit across 12 heel sts, pick up and knit 9 sts along side of heel flap; N2: work 22 instep sts in pat; N3: pick up and knit 9 sts along other side of heel flap, knit across 6 heel sts from N1; mark center back heel as beg of rnd—52 sts.

Rnd 1: N1: knit to last 3 sts, k2tog, k1; N2: work instep sts; N3: k1, ssk, knit to end.

Rnd 2: Work even in established pat.

Rep Rnds 1 and 2 until 40 sts rem.

Foot

Work even in pat until foot measures approx 2 inches less than desired length.

Toe

Change to St st.

Rnd 1: N1: knit to last 3 sts, k2tog, k1; N2: k1, ssk, knit to last 3 sts, k2tog, k1; N3: k1, ssk, knit to end.

Rnd 2: Knit around.

Rep Rnds 1 and 2 until 8 sts rem.

Divide sts evenly between 2 needles. Weave toe sts tog using Kitchener st, page 6. ●

Fun & Funky Booties

Design by Scarlet Taylor

Skill Level

 EASY

Sizes

Infant's 3–6 (6–9) months

Instructions are given for smallest size, with larger size in parentheses. When only 1 number is given, it applies to both sizes.

Finished Measurement

Sole: 3¾ (4¼) inches

Materials
- DK weight yarn (100% acrylic; 575 yds/7 oz per skein): 1 skein each blue (A) and lime (B)
- Size 6 (4mm) needles or size needed to obtain gauge
- 1 yd ⅜-inch-wide ribbon

Gauge

24 sts and 32 rows = 4 inches/10cm in St st.

To save time, take time to check gauge.

Special Abbreviation

Increase (inc): Inc 1 by knitting in front and back of next st on RS rows and purling in front and back of next st on WS rows.

Pattern Stitches

Stripe

In St st, work *2 rows A, 2 rows B; rep from * for pat.

1/1 Rib (even number of sts)

Row 1 (RS): *K1, p1; rep from * across.

Rep Row 1 for pat.

Booties

Sole

Note: *Work inc 1 st in from each side.*

With A, cast on 15 (18) sts.

Work Stripe pat in St st, inc 1 st each end [every row] 3 times, then [every RS row] once—23 (26) sts.

Continuing in Stripe pat work 3 (5) rows even.

Dec row (RS): K1, ssk, knit to last 3 sts, k2tog, k1—21 (24) sts.

Rep Dec row [every other row] once, then [every row] twice—15 (18) sts.

Bind off all sts.

Upper Section

Hold with RS facing; with A, pick up and knit 3 (5) sts from 1 short end of sole (for toe).

Toe

Row 1 and all WS rows: Purl across.

Row 2 (RS): K1, [inc] 2 (3) times, k0 (1)—5 (8) sts.

Row 4: K1 (2), [inc] 3 (4) times, k1 (2)—8 (12) sts.

Row 6: K2 (4), [inc] 5 times, k1 (3)—13 (17) sts.

Row 8: K4 (6), [inc] 6 times, k3 (5)—19 (23) sts.

Row 9: Purl across.

Rows 10–21: Work even in St st.

Row 22 (RS): K8 (10), bind off center 3 sts, knit rem sts.

First Side

Working on last 8 (10) sts, purl 1 row.

Dec row (RS): K1, ssk, k5 (7)—7 (9) sts.

Rep Dec row [every other row] twice—5 (7) sts.

Work 9 (10) rows even. Bind off all sts.

Second Side

Hold with WS facing; join A to rem 8 (10) sts, and purl 1 row.

Dec row (RS): Knit to last 3 sts, k2tog, k1—7 (9) sts.

Rep Dec row [every other row] twice—5 (7) sts.

Work 9 (10) rows even. Bind off all sts.

Edging

Hold with RS facing; with B, pick up and knit 28 (30) sts around ankle edge. Work in 1/1 Rib for approx ½ inch, ending with a WS row. Bind off loosely in ribbing.

Finishing

Sew heel seam. Sew sides of bootie and sole tog.

With 1 strand each of A and B held tog, make 2 small 1-inch pompoms for each bootie.

Cut ribbon in 2 (18-inch) lengths. Tie each length in bow. Referring to photo for placement, sew bow to bootie and then attach pompoms. ●

Pompoms

Cut two cardboard circles in size specified in pattern. Cut a hole in the center of each circle, about ½ inch in diameter. Thread a tapestry needle with a length of yarn doubled. Holding both circles together, insert needle through center hole, over the outside edge, and through center again (Fig. 1) until entire circle is covered and center hole is filled (thread more length of yarn as needed).

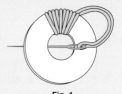

Fig. 1

With sharp scissors, cut yarn between the two circles all around the circumference. (Fig. 2)

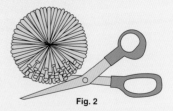

Fig. 2

Using two 12-inch strands of yarn, slip yarn between circles and overlap yarn ends 2 or 3 times

(Fig. 3) to prevent knot from slipping, pull tightly and tie into a firm knot.

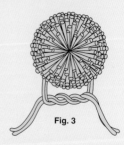

Fig. 3

Remove cardboard and fluff out pompom by rolling it between your hands. Trim even with scissors; leave the tying ends for when attaching pompom to project.

Arthur the Alien

Design by Penny Connor

Skill Level

◼◼◻◻ EASY

Finished Size

Height: Approx 9 inches (standing)

Finished Measurements

Chest: 27 (30½, 32, 34) inches

Length: 12 (15½, 17½, 19½) inches

Materials

- Worsted weight yarn (100% wool): small amounts green, blue, white, purple and orange, and ½ yd black (for mouth)
- Size 5 (3.75mm) needles or size needed to obtain gauge
- Stitch holder
- Polyester fiberfill
- Black felt
- Black thread and sewing needle
- Colored large-head straight pins

Gauge

Approx 22 sts and 30 rows = 4 inches/ 10cm in St st.

Exact gauge is not critical to this project, but it should be firm enough to prevent fiberfill from poking through.

Special Abbreviation

Make 1 (M1): Inc by making a backward loop over right needle.

Pattern Note

Refer to color key for specific colors to use and approximate yarn amounts needed for green or blue version.

Alien

Head

With A, leaving a 6-inch tail, cast on 9 sts.

Row 1 and all WS rows: Purl across.

Row 2 (RS): [K1, M1] 8 times, k1—17 sts.

Row 4: [K2, M1] 8 times, k1—25 sts.

Row 6: [K3, M1] 8 times, k1—33 sts.

Row 8: [K4, M1] 8 times—41 sts.

Rows 10–21: Beg with a knit row, work in St st.

Row 22: K1, [k2tog] 20 times—21 sts.

Row 24: K1, [k2tog] 10 times—11 sts.

Row 25: Purl across.

Cut yarn, leaving an 8-inch tail; thread end through rem 11 sts, pull tight and sew seam, leaving a 1½-inch opening to stuff head.

Run cast-on tail through cast-on sts, pull tight and fasten off. Stuff head firmly with fiberfill and complete seam.

Ear
Make 2

With D, leaving a 6-inch tail, cast on 5 sts.

Row 1 and all WS rows: Purl across.

Row 2 (RS): [K1, M1] 4 times, k1—9 sts.

Row 4: [K2, M1] 4 times, k1—13 sts.

Row 6: Knit across.

Row 8: K5, k3tog, k5—11 sts.

Row 10: K4, k3tog, k4—9 sts.

Row 12: K3, k3tog, k3—7 sts.

Row 14: Knit across.

Row 16: K2, k3tog, k2—5 sts.

Row 18: K1, k3tog, k1—3 sts.

Row 19: P3tog.

Cut yarn, leaving an 8-inch tail; fasten off. Sew seam, leaving a 1-inch opening to stuff. Stuff widest part of ear lightly with fiberfill and complete seam.

Eye
Make 3

With B, leaving a 6-inch tail, cast on 3 sts.

Row 1 and all WS rows: Purl across.

Row 2: [K1, M1] twice, k1—5 sts.

Row 4: [K1, M1] 4 times, k1—9 sts.

Row 6: Knit across.

Row 8: K1, [k2tog] 4 times—5 sts.

Row 10: K1, k3tog, k1—3 sts.

Row 11: P3tog.

Cut yarn, leaving a 6-inch tail; fasten off.

Place a small amount of fiberfill in each eye, and then tie 2 yarn tails tog tightly. Sew sides with 1 tail, and then tie ends tog again.

Referring to photo, cut 3 small semicircles from black felt for pupils; sew 1 on each eye using sewing needle and thread.

Body

Beg at bottom with A, leaving a 12-inch tail, cast on 9 sts.

Row 1 and all WS rows not given: Purl across.

Row 2 (RS): [K1, M1] 8 times, k1—17 sts.

Row 4: [K2, M1] 8 times, k1—25 sts.

Row 6: [K3, M1] 8 times, k1—33 sts.

Row 8: [K4, M1] 8 times, k1—41 sts.

Row 10: [K5, M1] 8 times, k1—49 sts.

Rows 12–16: Beg with a knit row, work in St st.

Row 17: Change to B; purl across.

Row 18: Purl across.

COLOR KEY			
	Green Alien	**Blue Alien**	**Approx Yardage**
A	Green	Blue	65 yds
B	White	White	25 yds
C	Purple	Orange	16 yds
D	Orange	Purple	16 yds
E	Blue	Green	12 yds

Row 19: Knit across.

Row 20: Change to C; knit across.

Row 22: Change to B; knit across.

Row 24: Change to E; knit across.

Row 26: Change to B; k7, ssk, k9, ssk, [k9, k2tog] twice, k7—45 sts.

Row 28: Change to C; knit across.

Row 30: Change to B; knit across.

Row 32: Change to E; knit across.

Row 34: Change to B; k7, ssk, k8, ssk, k7, k2tog, k8, k2tog, k7—41 sts.

Row 36: Change to C; knit across.

Row 38: K1, [k2tog] 20 times—21 sts.

Row 40: K1, [k2tog] 10 times—11 sts.

Bind off kwise. Cut yarn, leaving a 3-inch end; fasten off.

Using cast-on tail, run yarn through each cast-on st, pull tight and secure, gathering cast-on edge. Sew seam, leaving a 2-inch opening to stuff body. Stuff body firmly with fiberfill and complete seam, leaving bound-off edge open.

Left Arm

With C, leaving a 6-inch tail, cast on 15 sts.

Rows 1–7: Beg with a knit row, work in St st.

Row 8 (WS): Change to B; purl across.

Row 9: Purl across.

Row 10: Knit across.

Row 11: Change to A; knit across.

Row 12: Purl across.

Rows 13–20: Beg with a knit row, work in St st.

Finger

Row 21: K7, slip these 7 sts onto a holder; [k2, M1] 3 times, k2.

Note: There are now 7 sts on holder and 11 sts on main needle.

Row 22 and rem WS rows: Purl across.

Row 23: K5, M1, k1, M1, k5—13 sts.

Row 25: K5, k3tog, k5—11 sts.

Row 27: K4, k3tog, k4—9 sts.

Row 29: K3, k3tog, k3—7 sts.

Row 31: K1, [k2tog] 3 times—4 sts.

Cut yarn, leaving a 6-inch tail. Run yarn through rem 4 sts, pull tight and leave for later.

Thumb

Transfer 7 sts from holder to needle.

With WS facing, attach A and purl across.

Next 6 rows: Beg with a knit row, work in St st.

Cut yarn, leaving an 8-inch tail; thread end through rem sts, pull yarn tight and sew thumb seam. Sew finger seam. Stuff finger and sew arm seam, stuffing lightly before closing seam. Using cast-on tail, gather cast-on sts tog, pull tight and fasten off.

Right Arm

Work Rows 1–20 as for left arm.

Thumb

Row 21: [K2, M1] 3 times, k2, slip these 11 sts onto a holder; knit rem 7 sts.

Row 22 (WS): P7.

Rows 23–28: Beg with a knit row, work in St st.

Cut yarn, leaving a 6-inch tail; thread end through rem sts, pull yarn tight and sew thumb seam, leave for later.

Finger

Transfer 11 sts from holder to needle.

With WS facing, attach A and purl across. Work Rows 23–31 as for left arm finger—4 sts rem.

Cut yarn, leaving an 8-inch tail; thread end through rem sts, pull yarn tight and sew finger seam. Complete as for left arm.

Leg
Make 2

With D, leaving an 8-inch tail, cast on 7 sts.

Row 1: Knit across.

Row 2: [K1, M1] 6 times, k1—13 sts.

Row 3: Knit across.

Row 4: [K1, M1] 12 times, k1—25 sts.

Rows 5–7: Knit across.

Row 8: Change to A; knit across.

Row 9 and rem WS rows: Purl across.

Row 10: Knit across.

Row 12: K11, k3tog, k11—23 sts.

Row 14: K10, k3tog, k10—21 sts.

Row 16: K6, [k3tog] 3 times, k6—15 sts.

Rows 18–25: Beg with a knit row, work in St st.

Row 26: K2, ssk, k7, k2tog, k2—13 sts.

Row 28: Knit across.

Row 30: K2, ssk, k5, k2tog, k2—11 sts.

Row 32: Knit across.

Row 34: K1, [k2tog] 5 times—6 sts.

Cut yarn, leaving a 6-inch end; thread yarn through rem needles, pull tight. Using cast-on tail, gather cast-on sts tog, pull tight and fasten securely. Sew leg seam, stuffing leg and foot firmly with fiberfill before completing seam.

Assembly

Note: *Designer suggests pinning pieces in place, using pins with large, colored heads, so you can easily check to make sure all pins have been removed.*

Referring to photo, sew head to body, and then ears and eyes on head. Sew arms and legs to body. Using black yarn, embroider mouth on face. ●

Plum Berry Blanket & Pillow

Designs by Corrina Ferguson

Skill Level

INTERMEDIATE

Finished Measurements

Pillow: 18 inches x 12 inches

Blanket: 48 inches wide x 36 (48, 60) inches long

Blanket instructions are given for smallest size, with larger sizes in parentheses. When only 1 number is given, it applies to all sizes.

Materials

- King Cole Big Value Super Chunky (super bulky; 100% premium acrylic; 90 yds/100g per skein): 7 (8, 9) skeins grey #24 (MC) and 2 (3, 4) skeins bramble #1978 (CC)
- Size 15 (10mm) 40-inch circular needle or size needed to obtain gauge
- 12 x 18-inch pillow form
- 2 stitch markers

Gauge

10 sts and 16 rows = 4 inches/10cm in Lattice st.

To save time, take time to check gauge.

Special Abbreviation

Slip marker (sm): Slip marker from LH needle to RH needle.

Pattern Stitches

Note: Charts are included for those preferring to work sl st pats from a chart.

1-Color Lattice (multiple of 6 sts + 10)

Row 1 (RS): K2, sl 1, *k4, sl 2; rep from * to last 7 sts, k4, sl 1, k2.

Row 2 (WS): P2, sl 1, *p4, sl 2; rep from * to last 7 sts, p4, sl 1, p2.

Row 3: Rep Row 1.

Row 4: K2, sl 1, *k4, sl 2; rep from * to last 7 sts, k4, sl 1, k2.

Row 5: K4, sl 2, *k4, sl 2; rep from * to last 4 sts, k4.

Row 6: P4, sl 2, *p4, sl 2; rep from * to last 4 sts, p4.

Row 7: Rep Row 5.

Row 8: K4, sl 2, *k4, sl 2; rep from * to last 4 sts, k4.

Rep Rows 1–8 for pat.

2-Color Lattice (multiple of 6 sts + 10)

Row 1 (RS, CC): K2, sl 1, *k4, sl 2; rep from * to last 7 sts, k4, sl 1, k2.

Row 2 (WS, CC): P2, sl 1, *p4, sl 2; rep from * to last 7 sts, p4, sl 1, p2.

Row 3 (MC): Rep Row 1.

Row 4 (MC): K2, sl 1, *k4, sl 2; rep from * to last 7 sts, k4, sl 1, k2.

Row 5 (CC): K4, sl 2, *k4, sl 2; rep from * to last 4 sts, k4.

Row 6 (CC): P4, sl 2, *p4, sl 2; rep from * to last 4 sts, p4.

Row 7 (MC): Rep Row 5.

Row 8 (MC): K4, sl 2, *k4, sl 2; rep from * to last 4 sts, k4.

Rep Rows 1–8 for pat.

Pattern Notes

Blanket and pillow are both worked flat.

Blanket uses 2 colorwork methods: slipped stitches for the 2-Color Lattice pattern and intarsia for the borders worked in main color.

When changing colors, pick up new yarn under old to prevent holes.

Carry yarn not in use loosely up inside of garter border.

Long circular needles are recommended for the large number of stitches in the blanket; do not join, work back and forth in rows.

Slip all stitches in Lattice patterns purlwise with yarn on wrong side of work.

Pillow

With MC, cast on 46 sts.

Work in 1-Color Lattice pat for 12 inches, then work in garter st for 12 inches.

Bind off all sts loosely.

Finishing

Weave in ends.

Sew up 1 short end of pillow sleeve, then sew long edges tog.

Insert pillow form.

Sew final short end closed.

Weave in ends.

Blanket

With MC, cast on 102 sts.

Slipping first st of each row pwise wyif, knit 9 rows.

Next row (WS): Sl 1, k9, pm, knit to last 10 sts, pm, k10.

2-Color Center

Setup row (RS): With MC, sl 1, k9, sm, then join CC and work Row 1 of 2-Color Lattice pat to next marker, join a new ball of MC, knit to end.

Continue in this manner, slipping first st of each row pwise wyif, working MC borders in garter st and working center sts in 2-Color Lattice pat.

Note: Use first ball of MC for right border and Lattice pat; continue to use 2nd ball of MC for left border.

Work until blanket measures approx 32 (44, 56) inches from cast-on edge, ending with either Row 3 or Row 7 of 2-Color Lattice pat.

Cut CC and extra ball of MC.

Using MC and slipping first st of each row pwise wyif, knit 10 rows.

Bind off all sts loosely.

Finishing

Weave in all ends.

Block lightly. ●

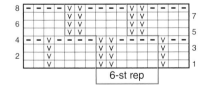

1-COLOR LATTICE PAT CHART

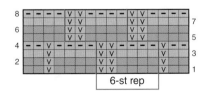

2-COLOR LATTICE PAT CHART

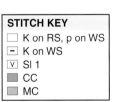

STITCH KEY
☐ K on RS, p on WS
─ K on WS
Ⅴ Sl 1
▓ CC
▒ MC

Lemon Ice Dishcloth

Design by Lisa Carnahan

Skill Level

 INTERMEDIATE

Finished Measurement

10 inches square

Materials

- Worsted weight yarn (100% cotton): 1 ball ivory
- Size 7 (4.5mm) needles or size needed to obtain gauge
- Cable needle

Gauge

17 sts = 4 inches/10cm in St st.

To save time, take time to check gauge.

Special Abbreviations

Left purl cross (LPC): Slip next st to cn and hold in front, p1, k1 from cn.

Right purl cross (RPC): Slip next st to cn and hold in back, k1, p1 from cn.

Pattern Stitch

Lemon Ice (multiple of 4 sts + 2)

Note: A chart is provided for those preferring to work pat st from a chart.

LEMON ICE CHART

STITCH KEY
☐ K on RS, p on WS
⊟ P on RS, k on WS
⧄⧅ RPC
⧅ LPC

Row 1 (WS): K1, *k1, p2, k1; rep from * to last st, k1.

Row 2 (RS): K1, *RPC, LPC; rep from * to last st, k1.

Row 3: K1, *p1, k2, p1; rep from * to last st, k1.

Row 4: K1, *k1, p2, k1; rep from * to last st, k1.

Row 5: Rep Row 3.

Row 6: K1, *LPC, RPC; rep from * to last st, k1.

Row 7: Rep Row 1.

Row 8: K1, *p1, k2, p1; rep from * to last st, k1.

Rep Rows 1–8 for pat.

Dishcloth

Cast on 54 sts.

Rep Rows 1–8 of Lemon Ice pat until piece measures approx 10 inches.

Bind off kwise. ●

Mixed Sherbet Dishcloth

Design by Lisa Carnahan

Skill Level

 EASY

Finished Measurement

10 inches square

Materials

- Worsted weight yarn (100% cotton): 1 ball orange/yellow/green variegated
- Size 7 (4.5mm) needles or size needed to obtain gauge

Gauge

17 sts = 4 inches/10cm in St st.

To save time, take time to check gauge.

Pattern Note

Increase by knitting in front and back of next stitch. Decrease by knitting 2 stitches together.

Dishcloth

Cast on 42 sts.

Border

Rows 1 and 2: Knit.

Row 3: Knit across and inc 6 sts evenly spaced—48 sts.

Body

Row 1 (RS): K2, *yo, k2, pass yo over k2 and off RH needle; rep from * to last 2 sts, k2.

Row 2: K2, purl to last 2 sts, k2.

Rep Rows 1 and 2 until piece measures about 9½ inches, ending with a RS row.

Border

Row 1: Knit across and dec 6 sts evenly spaced—42 sts.

Rows 2 and 3: Knit.

Bind off kwise. ●

Olive Ladders Dishcloth

Design by Lisa Carnahan

Skill Level

◼◼◻◻ EASY

Finished Measurement

10 inches square

Materials

- Worsted weight yarn (100% cotton): 1 ball olive
- Size 7 (4.5mm) needles or size needed to obtain gauge

Gauge

17 sts = 4 inches/10cm in St st.

To save time, take time to check gauge.

Pattern Stitch

Ladders (multiple of 8 sts + 5)

Note: A chart is provided for those preferring to work pattern from a chart.

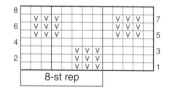

LADDERS CHART

STITCH KEY
☐ K on RS, p on WS
Ⅴ Slip pwise wyif on RS, slip pwise wyib on WS

Row 1 (RS): K5, *sl 3 pwise wyif, k5; rep from * across.

Row 2: *P5, sl 3 pwise wyib; rep from * to last 5 sts, p5.

Row 3: Rep Row 1.

Row 4: Purl across.

Row 5: K1, sl 3 pwise wyif, k1, *k4, sl 3 pwise wyif, k1; rep from * across.

Row 6: *P1, sl 3 pwise wyib, p4; rep from * to last 5 sts, p1, sl 3 pwise wyib, p1.

Row 7: Rep Row 5.

Row 8: Purl across.

Rep Rows 1–8 for pat.

Dishcloth

Cast on 45 sts. Purl 1 row.

Rep Rows 1–8 of Ladders pat until piece measures approx 10 inches, ending with Row 3 or Row 7.

Bind off pwise. ●

Cobblestones Dishcloth

Design by Lisa Carnahan

Skill Level

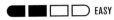 EASY

Finished Measurement

10 inches square

Materials

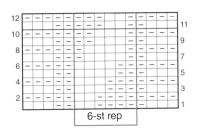

- Worsted weight yarn (100% cotton): 1 ball red
- Size 7 (4.5mm) needles or size needed to obtain gauge

Gauge

17 sts = 4 inches/10cm in St st.

To save time, take time to check gauge.

Pattern Note

Increase by knitting in front and back of next stitch. Decrease by knitting 2 stitches together.

Pattern Stitch

Cobblestones (multiple of 6 sts + 9)

Note: A chart is provided for those preferring to work pat st from a chart.

COBBLESTONES CHART

STITCH KEY
☐ K on RS, p on WS
⊟ P on RS, k on WS

Row 1 (RS): K3, p1, *p4, k2; rep from * to last 5 sts, p2, k3.

Row 2 and all WS rows: K3, knit the knits and purl the purls across to last 3 sts, k3.

Row 3: K3, p1, *p3, k3; rep from * to last 5 sts, p2, k3.

Row 5: K3, p1, *p2, k4; rep from * to last 5 sts, p2, k3.

Row 7: K3, p1, *p1, k4, p1; rep from * to last 5 sts, p2, k3.

Row 9: K3, p1, *p1, k3, p2; rep from * to last 5 sts, p2, k3.

Row 11: K3, p1, *p1, k2, p3; rep from * to last 5 sts, p2, k3.

Row 12: K3, knit the knits and purl the purls to last 3 sts, k3.

Rep Rows 1–12 for pat.

Dishcloth

Cast on 42 sts.

Border

Rows 1–4: Knit.

Row 5 (WS): Knit and inc 3 sts evenly across—45 sts.

Row 6 (RS): K3, purl to last 3 sts, k3.

Row 7: Knit.

Body

Rep Rows 1–12 of Cobblestones pat until piece measures approx 9 inches.

Border

Row 1 (RS): K3, purl to last 3 sts, k3.

Row 2: Knit.

Row 3: Knit and dec 3 sts evenly spaced across—42 sts.

Rows 4–6: Knit.

Bind off kwise. ●

Double-Knitted Hot Pad & Coasters

Designs by Carri Hammett

Skill Level

■■■□□ EASY

Finished Measurements

Pot holder: 7 inches wide x 7½ inches long

Coaster: 3¾ inches square

Materials

- Worsted weight yarn (100% cotton): 99 yds/2 oz each purple (A) and green (B)
- Size 7 (4.5mm) straight and double-point needles or size needed to obtain gauge

Gauge

15 sts and 22 rows = 4 inches/10cm in double-knit St st.

To save time, take time to check gauge.

Pattern Note

Review Double-Take Knitting article on page 40 before starting.

Hot Pad

With A, cast on 52 sts.

Join B and work Rows 1–39 of chart. Cut B.

Using 2 dpns, transfer sts alternately so that each color is on its own needle.

With A, join using 3-needle bind-off (see page 41).

Coasters

Green-Border Coaster

With B, cast on 28 sts.

Join A and work Rows 1–19 of chart. Cut A.

Transfer sts onto 2 dpns as for pot holder.

With B, work 3-needle bind-off.

Purple-Border Coaster

With A, cast on 28 sts.

Join B and work Rows 1–19 of chart.

Cut yarn B.

Transfer sts onto 2 dpns as for pot holder.

With A, work 3-needle bind-off.

Finishing

Weave in ends.

*Steam-block all edges so that sts lay flat.

Sew edges tog using blanket st and contrasting color. ●

COLOR & STITCH KEY
- ■ RS—k with A, p with B
- ■ WS—k with B, p with A
- ■ RS—k with B, p with A
- ■ WS—k with A, p with B

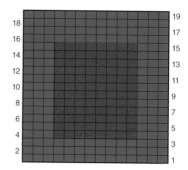

GREEN-BORDER COASTER CHART

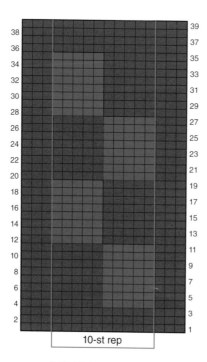

10-st rep

POT HOLDER CHART

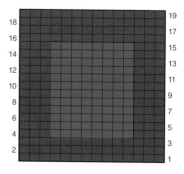

PURPLE-BORDER COASTER CHART

See pages 40 & 41 for Double-Take Knitting tutorial.

Double-Take Knitting

By Carri Hammett

Double knitting is often used to produce extra-warm hats and scarves, but it's also ideal for making thick pot holders and coasters. Typically, two yarns of different colors are used. The color on one side appears in opposite locations to the color on the other side in the finished project. The colors can be switched for a whole row to make stripes or switched periodically across a row to make any number of colorwork patterns without strands or floats as seen with Fair Isle knitting.

Getting Started

For double knitting, an even number of stitches should be cast on, and the total should be twice as many as needed for the width of the finished project. To practice, you will need two colors of yarn, A (purple in sample project) and B (green in sample project). Familiarize yourself with the technique by working with just one yarn first. Cast on 20 stitches using yarn A and work a couple rows as follows:

*Knit 1, slip 1 with yarn in front; repeat from * to end.

Notice how both the front and the back look identical, and the knitted fabric has two layers.

Now, for the fun part—double knitting with two colors. Begin by joining B and then working across the row as follows:

With both yarns held at the back, knit 1 with B.

Next, bring both yarns to the front and purl 1 with A.

Return both yarns to the back and knit 1 with B.

Continue in this manner, alternating between a knit stitch with B and a purl stitch with A to the end of the row. Remember to move both strands of yarn to the back to make the knit stitch and to the front to make the purl stitch. When you reach the end of the row, half of the stitches—the ones in front—will have been knit with B, and half of the stitches—the ones in back—will have been purled with A.

The second row is the opposite of the first:

*With yarn in back, knit 1 using A; with yarn in front, purl 1 using B; repeat from * to end.

After a few rows you can see that each side is a different color.

Creating colorwork patterns is easily accomplished by switching the two yarns as follows:

[With yarn in back, knit 1 using B; with yarn in front, purl 1 using A] 5 times; switch the position of the yarns by twisting them; [with yarn in back, knit 1 using A; with yarn in front, purl 1 using B] 5 times.

The directions for the next row are the same (since the colors were switched halfway across the row).

Double-Knitting Charts

Reading double-knitting charts is easy as long as you understand that each square on a chart represents two stitches. Also, remember that the chart shows only one side of the work, and that Row 1 is read from right to left and Row 2 is read from left to right. Shown below is a chart that represents the color changes on the sample swatch.

On Side 1 (odd-numbered) rows, knit 1 with the color shown on chart and purl 1 with the opposite color. On Side 2 (even-numbered) rows, knit 1 with the color opposite what is shown on chart followed by a purl 1 with the color shown on chart. So, the directions for the first two rows of the chart above are:

Row 2 [chart] Row 1

COLOR KEY
■ A
■ B

Row 1: [Wyib, k1 B; wyif, p1 A] 5 times, [wyib, k1 A; wyif, p1 B] 5 times.

Row 2: Rep Row 1.

Binding Off With Double Knitting

There are a number of ways to bind off in double knit, but I prefer using the 3-needle bind-off (see illustration).

Begin by placing all the front stitches on one needle and the back stitches on another. Use a third needle to work a 3-needle bind-off.

You will notice that the sides of the knitting are open in the areas that used two different yarns. This can be remedied by twisting the yarns around each other when starting a new row (bring the working yarn underneath). I don't like the way the stitches look when the yarns are twisted, so I work a decorative blanket stitch to join the sides instead.

Thread about 36 inches of yarn into a yarn needle and make a knot. Begin by making a small stitch on the wrong side so the needle exits at the edge of the work. Next move about ¼ to the right and make a small stitch. Keep the working yarn behind the needle as the stitch is made. Pull the yarn firmly, removing any slack from the strand on the edge.

Continuing to work to the right, make small even stitches around the entire edge.

The best way to deal with the corners is to make three stitches using the same entrance hole.

Once you've mastered the basics, I encourage you to learn more about this fun technique and get used to your double knitting getting double takes! ●

3-Needle Bind-Off

Use this technique for seaming two edges together, such as when joining a shoulder seam. Hold the edge stitches on two separate needles with right sides together.

With a third needle, knit together a stitch from the front needle with one from the back.

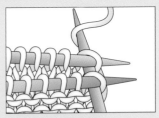

Repeat, knitting a stitch from the front needle with one from the back needle once more.

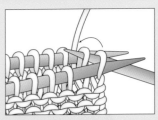

Slip the first stitch over the second.

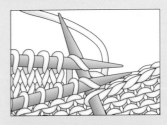

Repeat knitting, a front and back pair of stitches together, then bind one off.

Make Your Mug Happy

Designs by Lena Skvagerson for Annie's Signature Designs

Skill Level
Confident Beginner

Finished Measurements
Rug: 7 inches wide x 8½ inches long (not including fringe)

Cozy: 4 inches tall x 9¼ inches in circumference at top

Note: *Cozy fits a large to-go cup.*

Materials

- Chunky weight yarn (60% acrylic/40% nylon): 116 yds/100g each medium purple (A), pink (B), leaf green (C), light purple (D), aqua (E), blue (F), white (G) and lime green (H)
- Size 10 (6mm) needles or size needed to obtain gauge
- Size I/9 (5.5mm) crochet hook (to apply fringe)

Gauge
14 sts and 28 rows = 4 inches/10cm in Tweed pat.

16 sts and 18 rows = 4 inches/10cm in Gingham pat.

18 sts and 18 rows = 4 inches/10cm in Daisy pat.

To save time, take time to check gauge.

Special Abbreviations
Daisy Stitch (DS): P3tog, but don't slip new st from needle; yo, then purl same 3 sts tog again; slip them from needle.

Centered Double Decrease (CDD): Slip 2 sts as if to k2tog, k1, p2sso to dec 2 sts.

Pattern Note
Slip all stitches purlwise with yarn held to the wrong side of work.

Tweed Rug
With A, cast on 23 sts.

Knit 1 row.

Work in Tweed pat as follows:

Row 1 (RS): With B, k3, [sl 1, k3] 5 times.

Row 2: With B, k3, [sl 1, k3] 5 times.

Row 3: With A, k1, [sl 1, k3] 5 times, sl 1, k1.

Row 4: With A, k1, [sl 1, k3] 5 times, sl 1, k1.

Rep Rows 1–4 until piece measures 8 inches, ending with Row 2.

With A, knit 2 rows.

Bind off.

Edges
With RS facing and A, pick up and knit approx 30 sts evenly along side edge.

Bind off kwise.

Rep on opposite side.

Finishing
Weave in ends.

Fringe
Cut approx 40 (6-inch-long) strands of B; holding 2 strands tog, attach single-knot fringe (see page 79) ¾ inch apart along top and bottom edges.

Gingham Rug
With C, cast on 26 sts.

Knit 1 row.

Work Gingham pat as follows:

Row 1 (RS): With D, k1, sl 1, [k2, sl 2] 5 times, k2, sl 1, k1.

Row 2: With D, p1, sl 1, [p2, sl 2] 5 times, p2, sl 1, p1.

Row 3: With C, knit.

Row 4: With E, p2, [sl 2, p2] 6 times.

Row 5: With E, k2, [sl 2, k2] 6 times.

Row 6: With C, purl.

Rep Rows 1–6 until piece measures 8 inches, ending with Row 3.

With C, knit 1 row.

Bind off all sts, leaving last st on needle; do not cut yarn. Turn piece to work along side edge.

With C, work edges as for Tweed Rug.

Weave in ends, then, using E, finish with fringe as for Tweed Rug.

Daisy Rug
With F, cast on 29 sts.

Knit 1 row.

Work Daisy pat as follows:

Row 1 (RS): With F, knit.

Row 2: With F, k1, [DS, k1] 7 times.

Row 3: With G, knit.

Row 4: With G, k1, p1, k1, [DS, k1] 6 times, p1, k1.

Rows 5 and 6: With H, rep Rows 1 and 2.

Rows 7 and 8: With F, rep Rows 3 and 4.

Rows 9 and 10: With G, rep Rows 1 and 2.

Rows 11 and 12: With H, rep Rows 3 and 4.

Rep Rows 1–12 until piece measures approx 8 inches, ending with Row 2 or 8 (a WS row with F).

With F, purl 1 row.

Bind off.

With F, work edges as for Tweed Rug.

Weave in ends, then, using H, finish with fringe as for Tweed Rug.

Afghan Cozy

Note: *Cozy is worked flat from top down, then seamed.*

With A, cast on 51 sts.

Row 1 (RS): With A, k1, ssk, [k9, CDD] 3 times, k9, k2tog, k1—43 sts.

Row 2: With A, k1, [p1, k4, (k1, yo, k1) in next st, k4] 4 times, p1, k1—51 sts.

Rows 3 and 4: With D, rep Rows 1 and 2.

Rows 5 and 6: With H, rep Rows 1 and 2.

Row 7: With A, k1, sk2p, [k6, ssk, sl 2 tog kwise, k2tog, p2sso] 3 times, k6, ssk, k2tog, k1—35 sts.

Row 8: With A, k1, [p1, k3, (k1, yo, k1) in next st, k3] 4 times, p1, k1—43 sts.

Row 9: With D, k1, ssk, [k7, CDD] 3 times, k7, k2tog, k1—35 sts.

Row 10: With D, rep Row 8—43 sts.

Rows 11 and 12: With H, rep Rows 9 and 10.

Rows 13 and 14: With A, rep Rows 9 and 10.

Bind off.

Finishing

Weave in ends.

Sew sides tog using mattress stitch, being sure to seam tog along the side of vertical column of knit sts. ●

Mattress Stitch